THE PASTOR'S INTERCESSOR

Dr. Aaron R. Jones

THE PASTOR'S INTERCESSOR

Published by
Kingdom Publishing, LLC
Odenton, Maryland

Printed in
The United States of America

Copyright © 2011 Dr. Aaron Jones

All scripture quotations are from the King James Version of the Bible. Thomas Nelson Publishers, Nashville: Thomas Nelson, Inc. 1972.

ISBN: 978-1-967006-04-5

Library of Congress Control Number: 2011917774

Editors: Sharon Jones and Terri Haynes
Typesetters: Juanita Banks and Terri J. Haynes

Table of Contents

FOREWORD

"And I will give you pastors according to mine heart, which shall feed you with knowledge and understanding."
Jeremiah 3:15

A book of this magnitude is well overdue. Pastors who operate according to the heart of God extend themselves beyond their physical and emotional strength. They spend hours preparing for ministry in all aspects of the lives of the people. They constantly desire to have the heart of God.

Jesus asked Peter three times if he loved him. Each time Peter answered, "Yes." Jesus told Peter, "Feed My sheep." This was a command and not a request. With this command, pastors are indebted to Jesus to carry out this command and to say "yes" to Jesus. When this book is read, it covers every aspect of the pastor's life. Intercessors are needed in the lives of the pastors.

In writing this book, Doctor Jones has the heart of a pastor. I am sure it is his desire that every pastor will have intercessors and that every pastor's ministry will be covered by prayer.

Pastor ViCurtis Little
Greater Deliverance Christian Center Church

Introduction

The call of every church member is to be an intercessor for his or her pastor. Hebrews 13:7 says, *"Remember them which have the rule over you, who have spoken unto you the word of God: whose faith follow, considering the end of their conversation."* How do we remember them? We pray for them. If we are to follow their faith, we must pray that our pastors keep the faith. The Bible is clear concerning the prayer for our leaders. I Timothy 2:1-2 says, *"I exhort therefore, that, first, supplications, prayers, intercessions, and giving of thanks, be made for all men. For kings, and for all that are in authority; that we may lead a quiet and peaceable life in all godliness and honesty."*

The attack on pastors grows daily; and intercessory prayer for all pastors is vital. I believe many saints do not pray for their pastor, because they have not truly considered the role of the pastor. Many people do not know the weight that is on a pastor's shoulder. Most saints look at the pastor as the person who brings the Word of God every Sunday. In some cases, Christians have become insensitive to the work of their pastor. The pastor is responsible for everything that goes on in the church, and at the end of the day, it is the pastor who accounts for the good and the bad.

I Peter 5:2 and 3 indicates that the roles of a pastor are to feed the congregation and to have oversight over them. As a shepherd tends to his sheep; so should a pastor tend to God's sheep. A pastor's responsibility does not end with feeding and overseeing. A pastor is also a leader, an evangelist, a prophet, and a father/mother. Some believe the pastor should be an expert in all facets of life.

As you can see, there are so many reasons to pray for your pastor; and listed are just a few more reasons to pray: (1) It is a commandment of God; (2) He/she is accountable to God; (3) He/she needs to hear from God daily; (4) He/she provides you with needed spiritual food; (5) He/she is able to aid you in your Christian Walk; (6) He/she prays and fasts for you; (7) He/she has troubles just as other parishioners; (8) The enemy is trying to destroy him/her daily; and (9) The weight that is on his/her shoulder. My prayer is that congregants do not fall in Satan's trap and not pray for their pastors.

There are additional reasons why parishioners do not pray for their pastors: (1) Some are so focused on their own personal ministry that they don't take the time to lift up the pastor; (2) Some feel the pastor does not need prayer, because he/she is the pastor; (3) Some are jealous of the pastor; (4) Some just don't like the pastor; (5) Some don't know how to intercede for the pastor; (6) Some have a negative perception of pastors; (7) Some are angry with their pastor; (8) Some do not want to see the pastor prosper; (9) Some do not see their pastor as the leader; and (10) Some do not agree with the vision. I have developed relevant thoughts to lead you into daily intercession for your pastor. Pastors need our prayers in all facets of his/her life. Your pastor needs the same intercession that is needed for your daily life's challenges. Will you pray? Join me in praying for your pastor.

"Pastor Aaron Jones gives us a candid look at intercession from the Pastor's point of view while taking prayer a step further. It is a deeply motivating glance into the life and challenges of pastorship. It encourages us to remove the limitations when praying for Leaders. I challenge you to read this book and learn to pray prayers that truly availes much!"

-Dr. Wanda J. Sisco Senior Pastor and Founder Beyond the Veil Worship Center

"Amazingly, Dr. Jones has earned a place in the heart of every pastor by speaking to the need that, for many of our local church leaders, has gone uncovered; intercession for the Pastor. In his book, 'The Pastors Intercessor: Devotional Prayers for your Pastor', This author slays two birds with one stone. He provides instruction by way of actual prayers for pastors while at the same time laying out key areas that churches must identify as battlegrounds for their leaders. This needs to be in the library of every Pastor's Aid Ministry, Armour Bearers group, and Deacons board."

-Pastor L. Frazier White II Faith Tabernacle UHCA Washington, D.C.

"The Pastor's Intercessor devotional is a powerful tool for the body of Christ! As I read the introduction, it was as if I was reading my own heart's cry. It made me think of 2 Chron. 7:14, which I see as God's heart's cry. While every prayer topic is vital to my very life as a pastor, the topics that touched me most were: "Pastor's Humility", Pastor's Patience", "Pastor's Trust In God", "Pastor's Vision'," Pastor's Family", "Pastor's Health", "Pastor's Troubles", and "Pastor's Favor." My prayer is that this devotional ends up not only in the hands of those called to the office of intercessor, but in the hands of every member of the body of Christ! I hear your heart-cry and pray that everyone who reads this book will answer the cry with prayer."

-Bishop Rick A. Felton

Senior Pastor Christian Love Church of God
"During a critical time in Christendom, whereby leaders and shepherds are under constant spiritual attack, this devotional is much needed and very timely. Dr. Jones has responded to the cry of many by establishing a prayer guide that will assist leaders in understanding how to effectively cover their Pastor in prayer. This devotional poignant, easy to read, and a necessary tool for daily use among leaders in the Kingdom of God."

-Elder Marc D. Talbert, Sr.
Senior Pastor Word of Life Christian Center

"This is a much-needed resource for church leaders and laity alike. Parishioners sometimes underestimate the importance and impact of fervent prayer for their Pastor. In this book, Dr. Jones does a great job relaying the message that--it's important to bathe your pastor in prayer!"

-Bishop James Izzard, Jr. Lead Pastor - Life Builders Christian Center

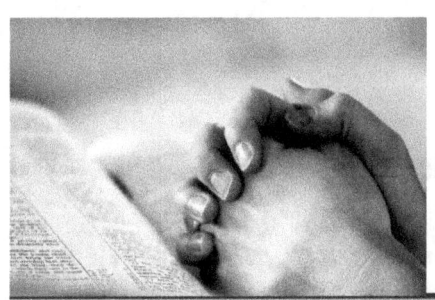

"Pray Without Ceasing"
I Thessalonians 5:17

The Pastor's Prayer Life

The Pastor's Prayer Life

The pastor must daily communicate with God; his prayer life is vital to the church, his family, and the work of the Lord. The pastor's communication with God becomes the source of how he ministers and maintains.

Supporting Scriptures

"But we will give ourselves continually to prayer, and to the ministry of the word."

Acts 6:4

"For God is my witness whom I serve with my spirit in the gospel of his Son, that without ceasing I make mention of you always in my prayers."

Romans 1:9

"And in the morning, rising up a great while before day, he (Jesus) went out, and departed into a solitary place, and there prayed."

Mark 1:35

Dear God,

I pray today that Pastor _____ stays fervent in prayer to the ministry of the Word; that Pastor _____ will continuously intercede for the Kingdom of God. Let Pastor be aware and intercede for the enemies of the ministry. Allow Pastor _____ to be intentional concerning quiet time with you. Thank you, God for Pastor _____. In Jesus name I pray, Amen.

Special Notes

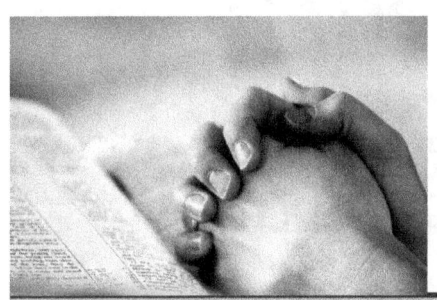

"Pray Without Ceasing"
I Thessalonians 5:17

The Pastor's Vision

The Pastor's Vision

God pours his vision into the pastor;
therefore, God's vision becomes the
pastor's. The vision from God is to guide
the local church and the body of Christ. The
vision is also to show the pastor revelation
of what God is doing in his life.

Supporting Scriptures

*"After these things the word of the Lord came unto
Abram in a vision, saying, Fear not, Abram: I
am thy shield and thy exceeding great reward."*
Genesis 15:1

"Where there is no vision, the people perish..."
Proverbs 29:18

*"For the vision is yet for an appointed time, but
at the end it shall speak, and not lie: though it*

tarry wait for it; because it will surely come, it will not tarry."

Habakkuk 2:3

Dear God,

Continue to pour fresh vision into Pastor _____. Open the eyes of our church to see what you are showing Pastor and let us be fully cooperative to carry out your will and plan. Keep Pastor _____ focused on your vision. I want to bind the assignment of the enemy to bring false vision to my Pastor. Thank you, God for Pastor _____. In Jesus name I pray, Amen

Special Notes

_____
_____
_____
_____
_____
_____
_____
_____
_____
_____
_____
_____
_____
_____
_____
_____
_____
_____
_____
_____
_____

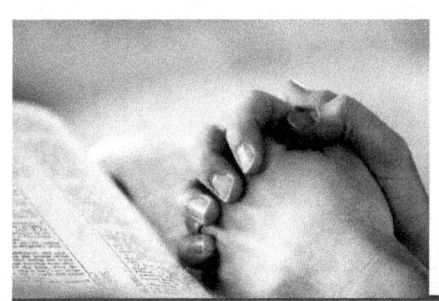

"Pray Without Ceasing"
I Thessalonians 5:17

The Pastor's Family

The Pastor's Family

God calls the pastor first to his family, because if the home of the pastor is not settled; it can potentially affect the pastor's ministry. Oftentimes, the enemy will use the family to get to the pastor.

Supporting Scriptures

"One that ruleth well his own house, having his children in subjection with all gravity; (For if a man know not how to rule his own house, how shall he take care of the church of God?)"
I Timothy 3:4, 5

"Children obey your parents in the Lord: for this is right."
Ephesians 6:1

"Husbands, love your wives, even as Christ, also loved the church, and gave himself for it."
Ephesians 5:25

Dear God,

I pray that Pastor   will see his/her home as important as God sees the home. Allow Pastor to always create an atmosphere of love in the home with his/her family. Let Pastor _____ children seek you and allow Jesus to be Lord of their lives. Let Pastor _____ family be the greatest example for our church. Thank you, God for Pastor _____ . In Jesus name I pray, Amen.

Special Notes

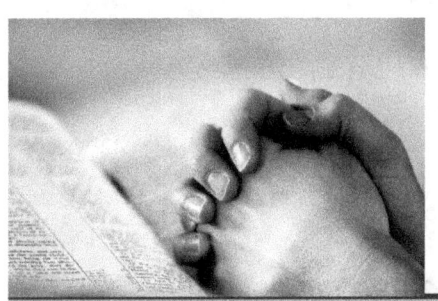

"Pray Without Ceasing"
I Thessalonians 5:17

The Pastor's Heart

The Pastor's Heart

The heart of the pastor should follow the heart of God, in other words, God's heartbeat should be the pastor's heartbeat. God wants a pastor whose heart remains willing for ministry and is compassionate to His people.

Supporting Scriptures

"Feed the flock of God which is among you, taking the oversight thereof, not by constraint, but willing..."

I Peter 5:2

"But when he saw the multitudes, he was moved with compassion on them, because they fainted, and were scattered abroad, as sheep having no shepherd."

Matthew 9:36

"But now thy kingdom shall not continue: the Lord hath sought him a man after his own heart, and the Lord hath commanded him to be captain over his people..."

I Samuel 13:14

Dear God,

Keep Pastor _____ heart in your hand, clean and renew it every day. Don't allow anything that doesn't please you to rest in Pastor _____ heart. God continue to grow compassion in Pastor _____ heart for your people, your purpose, and your plan. Let Pastor _____ heart be open to your desires. Thank you, God for Pastor _____. In Jesus name I pray, Amen.

Special Notes

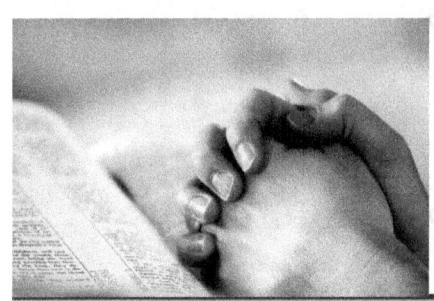

"Pray Without Ceasing"
I Thessalonians 5:17

The Pastor's Wisdom

The Pastor's Wisdom

One of the key sources of a successful pastorate is the use of Godly wisdom and counsel. The pastor must be constantly seeking wisdom from God. The wisdom of God will help a pastor find resolution in the toughest circumstances.

Supporting Scriptures

"Give therefore thy servant an understanding heart to judge my people, that I may discern between good and bad: for who is able to judge thy so great a people?"

I Kings 3:9

"If any man lack wisdom, let him ask of God, that giveth to all men liberally, and upbraideth not; and it shall be given him."

James 1:5

"Hearken now unto my voice, I will give thee counsel...Moreover thou shalt provide out of all the people able men, such as fear God, men of truth, hating covetousness; and place such over them, to be rulers of thousands, and rulers of hundreds, rulers of fifties, and rulers of tens."
Exodus 18:19, 21

Dear God,

Give Pastor _____ the wisdom needed to deal with the multitude of situations surrounding the church, home, and community. Surround him/her with godly men and women to give wise counsel, when it is needed: but also allow Pastor _____ to receive wise counsel. Stir up Pastor _____ to daily seek your wisdom. Thank you, God for Pastor _____. In Jesus name I pray, Amen.

Special Notes

"Pray Without Ceasing"
I Thessalonians 5:17

The Pastor's Will

The Pastor's Will

The will of God must remain the will of the pastor. God's desire is that the pastor operates in His will always. The pastor must daily seek the will of God for his life, as well as the life of the church.

Supporting Scriptures

"Jesus saith unto them, My meat is to do the will of him that sent me, and to finish his work."

John 4:34

"...O my Father, if it be possible, let this cup pass from me: nevertheless not as I will, but as thou will."

Matthew 26:39

"Thy kingdom come. Thy will be done in earth, as it is in heaven."

Matthew 6:10

Dear God,
Your thoughts and your ways are always higher than ours. Allow Pastor _____ to continuously seek your thoughts and ways to fulfill the ministry placed before him/her. Let your divine will always supersede what Pastor _____ may want. May the work of Pastor _____ hands be the meat of your kingdom. Thank you God for Pastor _____. In Jesus name I pray, Amen.

Special Notes

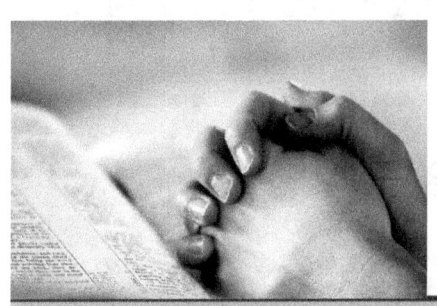

"Pray Without Ceasing"
I Thessalonians 5:17

The Pastor and Satan's Attacks

The Pastor and Satan's Attack

One of Satan's assignments among other things is to take out the pastor. He believes if the pastor can be tempted to fall into a sin, he has won. Satan will continue by any means necessary to remove the shepherd.

Supporting Scriptures

"And when the tempter came to him, he said, if thou be the Son of God, command that these stones be made bread. But He answered and said, it is written, man shall not live by bread alone, but by every word that proceedeth out of the mouth of God."

Matthew 4:3, 4

"No weapon that is formed against thee shall prosper..."

Isaiah 54:17

"The thief cometh not, but for to steal, and to kill, and to destroy..."

John 10:10

Dear God,

I pray that no weapon formed against Pastor _____ will prosper. Every assignment that Satan draws up is canceled right now in the name of Jesus. Daily strengthen Pastor _____ to resist the enemy and his attacks. Allow Pastor _____ to walk in victory. Thank you, God for Pastor _____. In Jesus name I pray, Amen.

Special Notes

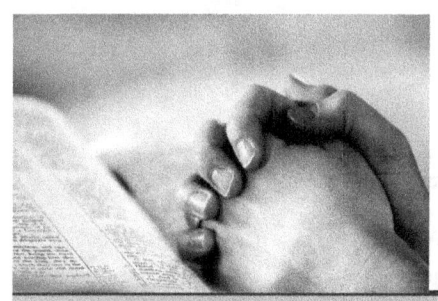

"Pray Without Ceasing"
I Thessalonians 5:17

The Pastor and the Holy Spirit

The Pastor and the Holy Spirit

When Jesus left this earth to go and be with the Father, He sent the Holy Spirit to help lead and guide the church. The Holy Spirit must be involved daily in the life of the pastor.

Supporting Scriptures

"Howbeit when he, the Spirit of truth, is come, he will guide you into all truth…"

John 16:13

"But the Comforter, which is the Holy Ghost, whom the Father will send in my name, he shall teach you all things, and bring all things to your remembrance, whatsoever I have said unto you."

John 14:26

"And they were all filled with the Holy Ghost, and began to speak with other tongues, as the Spirit gave them utterance."

Acts 2:4

Dear God,

Continue to lead and teach Pastor _____ in all truth. Guide Pastor _____ every step, directing and leading his/her heart. Bring all things you have showed Pastor _____ to remembrance in the times of need and ministry. May the Holy Spirit always be working through Pastor _____ to fulfill every assignment ordained for his/her watch. Thank you, God for Pastor _____. In Jesus name I pray, Amen.

Special Notes

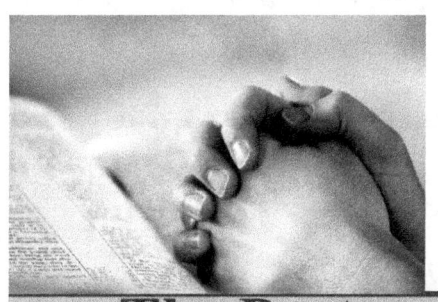

"Pray Without Ceasing"
I Thessalonians 5:17

The Pastor and Praise/ Worship

The Pastor and Praise/Worship

The pastor should set the tone for praise and worship in a church. Oftentimes, the church will take the lead from the pastor in praise and worship. The atmosphere of the pastor's praise and worship will set the tone of the church service.

Supporting Scriptures

"Give unto the Lord glory due unto his name: bring an offering and come before him: worship the Lord in the beauty of holiness."

I Chronicles 16:29

"I will bless the Lord at all times his praise shall continually be in my mouth."

Psalm 34:1

"Let every thing that hath breath praise the Lord. Praise ye the Lord."

Psalm 150:1

Dear God,

I pray that Pastor _____ gives all glory to you and always blesses you. Let Pastor _____ stay in your presence. Don't allow Pastor _____circumstances stop the flow of worship in the home, church, or in the community. Let Pastor _____ continuously praise you for his/her place of ministry. I thank you God for Pastor   . In Jesus name I pray, Amen

Special Notes

_____

_____

_____

_____

_____

_____

_____

_____

_____

_____

_____

_____

_____

_____

_____

_____

_____

_____

_____

_____

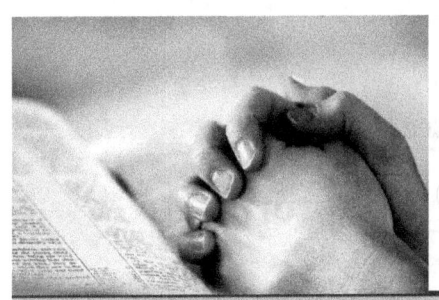

"Pray Without Ceasing"
I Thessalonians 5:17

The Pastor's Humility

The Pastor's Humility

One of the greatest characteristics of a leader is to be humble. Humility opens the door for growth in a pastor's life and ministry. Humility will keep the pastor's heart toward God and his mind on building God's kingdom.

Supporting Scriptures

"And whosoever shall exalt himself shall be abased; and he that shall humble himself shall be exalted."

Matthew 23:12

"Humble yourselves therefore under the mighty hand of God, that he may exalt you in due time."

I Peter 5:6

"Pride goeth before destruction, and a haughty spirit before a fall."

Proverbs 16:18

Dear God,

Keep Pastor _____ always humble before your presence. I speak against the spirit of pride in the life of Pastor _____; and I pray that Pastor _____ heart is never filled with pride. Let Pastor _____ learn to daily walk in humility and your grace. Thank you, God for Pastor _____. In Jesus name I pray, Amen.

Special Notes

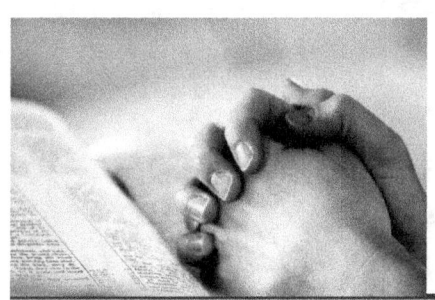

"Pray Without Ceasing"
I Thessalonians 5:17

The Pastor's Patience

The Pastor's Patience

With so many decisions a pastor must make, patience becomes crucial. The understanding of the work of patience and learning contentment will assist any pastor in not moving when God is saying "stay still."

Supporting Scriptures

"I wait for the Lord, my soul doth wait, and in his word do I hope."

Psalm 130:5

"And not only so, but we glory in tribulations also; knowing that tribulation worketh patience; and patience, experience; and experience, hope."

Romans 5:3, 4

"Not that I speak in respect of want: for I have learned, in whatsoever state I am, therewith to be content."

Philippians 4:11

Dear God,

Impress upon the heart of Pastor _____ the importance of patience and waiting on you. I pray that Pastor _____ will only move at your Word. I pray that Pastor _____ will master waiting on you. Thank you for Pastor _____. In the name of Jesus, Amen.

Special Notes

_____

_____

_____

_____

_____

_____

_____

_____

_____

_____

_____

_____

_____

_____

_____

_____

_____

_____

_____

_____

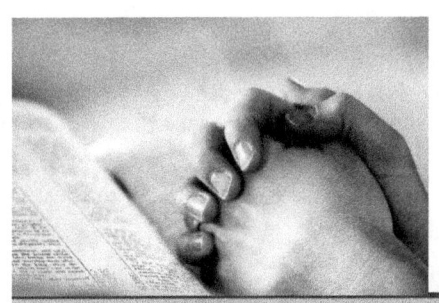

"Pray Without Ceasing"
I Thessalonians 5:17

The Pastor's Preaching and Teaching

The Pastor's Preaching and Teaching

The pastor is the mouthpiece for the plans and instructions of the Almighty God. Pray that your pastor's preaching and teaching is not based on enticing words of man's wisdom. Pray that your pastor is always prepared to give a word. Pray that your pastor's messages have free course. Pray that the gospel your pastor preaches is not catered to please man, but God. Pray that your pastor daily labors in the Word, so he can continue to feed the flock. Pray that the message your pastor delivers is received as truth

Supporting Scriptures

"And for me, that utterance may be given unto me, that I may open my mouth boldly, to make known the mystery of the gospel."

Ephesians 6:19

"And my speech and my preaching was not with enticing words of man's wisdom, but in demonstration of the Spirit and of power."
I Corinthians 2:4

"Finally, brethren, pray for us, that the word of the Lord may have free course, and be glorified, even as it is with you."
II Thessalonians 3:1

Dear God,

I pray that Pastor _____ will preach when preaching is not popular. Give Pastor _____ the courage and boldness to speak your truth in the pulpit. Open the hearts of those in our congregation to receive the instruction from you to Pastor _____. Allow Pastor _____ to apply your Word in his/her life and make it applicable for the lives of your children. Thank you for Pastor_____. In the name of Jesus, Amen.

Special Notes

"Pray Without Ceasing"
I Thessalonians 5:17

The Pastor's Trust in God

The Pastor's Trust in God

The pastor is looked upon to be all things to all men, and in some cases, he doesn't have a person to depend on. This makes trusting God so important, and the pastor's total dependence must be in God.

Supporting Scriptures

"In God I will praise his word, in God I have put my trust; I will not fear what flesh can do unto me."

Psalm 56:4

"Trust in the Lord with all thine heart; and lean not unto thine own understanding."

Proverbs 3:5

"Trust in the Lord, and do good; so shalt thou dwell in the land, and verily thou shalt be fed."

Psalm 37:3

Dear God,

I pray that Pastor _____ doesn't rely on man's wisdom and might but will trust in you each day. Increase Pastor _____ faith in you for the outcome of his/ her family, ministry, and the church. When it seems as if no one is there, let Pastor _____ remember you will not leave him/her under any circumstances. Thank you for Pastor _____. In Jesus name I pray, Amen.

Special Notes

"Pray Without Ceasing"
I Thessalonians 5:17

The Pastor's Christian Walk

The Pastor's Christian Walk

The pastor spends only minutes in a pulpit, but hours among people. The pastor's Christian walk is vital to the overall acceptance of pulpit ministry by the body of Christ. We must intercede for our pastors as it pertains to the daily disciplines of the Christian life. The call to bare fruit is just as important to the pastor as it is to a lay member of the church.

Supporting Scriptures

"Ye have not chosen me, but I have chosen you, and ordained you that ye should go and bring forth fruit..."

John 15:16

"Let your light so shine before men, that they may see your good works, and glorify your father which is in heaven"

Matthew 5:16

"The just man walketh in his integrity: his children are blessed after him."

Proverbs 20:7

Dear God,

Allow Pastor _____ to always be fruitful and to always let his/her light shine, especially outside the pulpit. Let Pastor _____ steps remain ordered in the Word.

I pray Pastor _____ lives a lifestyle of integrity and that he/she places him/herself in atmospheres which draw him/her closer to you. Thank you for Pastor _____. In Jesus name I pray, Amen

Special Notes

_____

_____

_____

_____

_____

_____

_____

_____

_____

_____

_____

_____

_____

_____

_____

_____

_____

_____

_____

_____

"Pray Without Ceasing"
I Thessalonians 5:17

The Pastor's Health

The Pastor's Health

The health of the pastor is so important to the effectiveness of ministry. The pastor must be intentional about taking time to refresh and relax.

Supporting Scriptures

"The apostles returned to Jesus, and told him all that they had done and taught, and he said to them, Come away by yourselves to a lonely place and rest a while. For many were coming and going, and they had no leisure even to eat. And they went away in the boat to a lonely place by themselves..."

Mark 6:30-32

"Beloved I wish above all things that thou mayest prosper and be in health, even as thy soul prospereth."

III John 1:2

"What? Know ye not that your body is the temple of the Holy Ghost which is in you, which ye have of God, and ye are not your own?"

I Corinthians 6:19

Dear God,

I pray Pastor _____ remains healthy daily. I bind all assignments of the enemy to bring sickness and disease on Pastor _____ life. I pray that Pastor _____ will eat the foods that will build his/her strength. I pray that you not only touch Pastor _____ body, but touch his/her family, and keep them free from sickness. Thank you for Pastor _____. In Jesus name I pray, Amen.

Special Notes

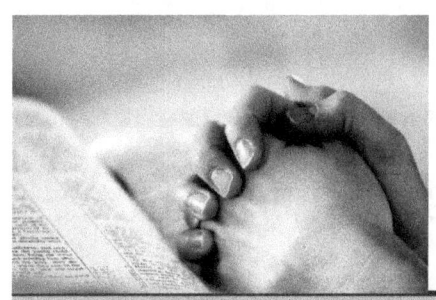

"Pray Without Ceasing"
I Thessalonians 5:17

The Pastor's Protection

The Pastor's Protection

The pastor travels on any given day. The enemy would love to destroy the pastor. Our pastors need the covering of angels daily. God wants to fight the pastor's battle.

Supporting Scriptures

"The angel of the Lord encampeth round about them that fear him, and delivereth them."
Psalm 34:7

"And Moses built an altar, and called the name of it Jehovah- nissi."
Exodus 17:15

"When the wicked, even mine enemies and my foes, came upon me to eat up my flesh, they stumbled and fell."
Psalm 27:2

Dear God,

Keep your angels around Pastor _____. I declare no weapon formed against Pastor _____ will prosper. Protect his/her mind and heart against the influences of the enemy. Allow every step of Pastor _____ to be covered by the blood Jesus. Thank you for Pastor _____. In the name of Jesus, Amen.

Special Notes

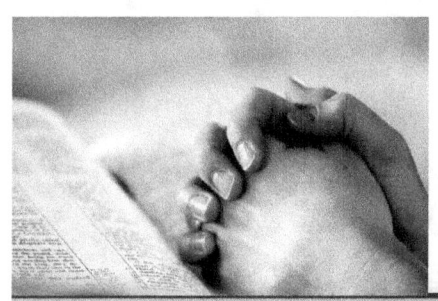

"Pray Without Ceasing"
I Thessalonians 5:17

The Pastor's Mind

The Pastor's Mind

The mind of the pastor must be focused at all times. Daily there will be situations, events, and decisions that will keep the mind of a pastor engaged. The pastor must make various decisions every day; these decisions may be as simple as the cleaning of the church to the life and death of a member.

Supporting Scriptures

"Finally, brethren, whatsoever things are true, whatsoever things are just, whatsoever things are pure, whatsoever things are lovely, whatsoever things are of good report; if there be any virtue, and if there be any praise, think on these things."
Philippians 4:8

"And be not conformed to this world: but be ye transformed by the renewing of your mind, that

ye may prove what is that good, and acceptable, and perfect, will of God."

Romans 12:2

"Let this mind be in you, which was also in Christ Jesus."

Philippians 2:5

Dear God,

Keep Pastor _____ mind focused and renewed daily. I bind any thoughts that are contrary to the Word, brought by Satan, to infiltrate Pastor _____ mind. I pray that Pastor _____ focuses his/her mind on things that edify, so his/her thoughts are aligned with you. Thank you for Pastor _____. In Jesus name I pray, Amen.

Special Notes

_____
_____
_____
_____
_____
_____
_____
_____
_____
_____
_____
_____
_____
_____
_____
_____
_____
_____
_____
_____

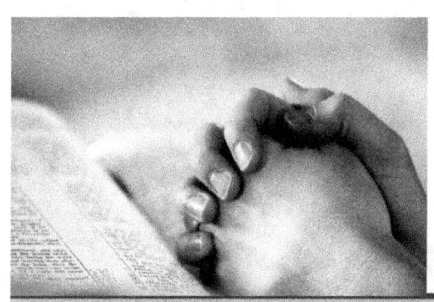

"Pray Without Ceasing"
I Thessalonians 5:17

The Pastor and Evangelism

The Pastor's Evangelism

The pastor must be the mouthpiece for evangelism from the pulpit. The pastor enforces the significance of God's Word being evangelized from house-to-house, city-to-city, and nation-to-nation.

Supporting Scriptures

"Then saith he unto his disciples, the harvest truly is plenteous, but the labourers are few."
Matthew 9:37

"For the Son of man is come to seek and to save that which is lost."
Luke 19:10

"And he said unto them, Go ye into all the world, and preach the gospel to every creature."
Mark 16:15

Dear God,

Give Pastor _____ the wisdom and knowledge to relay the significance of evangelism. Allow the words Pastor _____ uses to penetrate the heart of the congregation so that evangelism becomes a lifestyle. Let evangelism always be a part of the vision and mission of our church. Show Pastor _____ how to integrate evangelism in all ministries of our church. Thank you for Pastor _____. In the name of Jesus I pray, Amen.

Special Notes

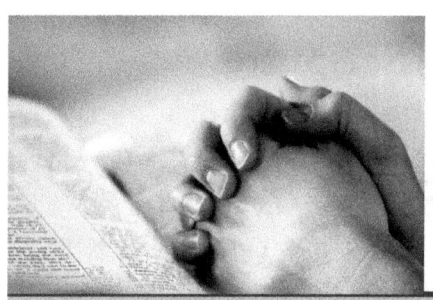

"Pray Without Ceasing"
I Thessalonians 5:17

The Pastor's Strength

The Pastor's Strength

The renewed strength of the pastor will help him survive the day. Being a pastor can be draining physically,

Supporting Scriptures

"And let us not be weary in well doing: for in due seasons we shall reap, if we faint not."
Galatians 6:9

"For as the suffering of Christ abound in us, so our consolation also aboundeth by Christ."
II Corinthians 1:5

"For which cause we faint not; but though our outward man perish, yet the inward man is renewed day by day."
II Corinthians 4:16

Dear God,

Strengthen Pastor _____ this day and do not allow him/ her to get weary while working in ministry. As the hard days come for Pastor _____, please give him/her the wherewithal to endure during times of suffering. Renew Pastor _____ from the crown of his/her head to the soles of his/her feet and renew the spirit man. Daily encourage Pastor _____ as he/she labors. Let this labor be all for your kingdom building. Thank you for Pastor _____. In Jesus name I pray, Amen.

Special Notes

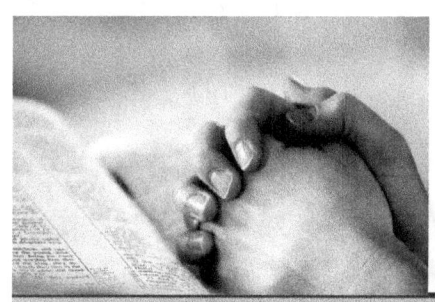

"Pray Without Ceasing"
I Thessalonians 5:17

The Pastor's Relationships

The Pastor's Relationships

Ministry is about relationships. Jesus is clear how mankind should get along with one another. The pastor's ministry is about relationships: relationship to God; relationship to family; relationship to leaders; relationship to community; and relationship to the church. The pastor must embrace relationships as Jesus did.

Supporting Scriptures

"Henceforth I call you not servants; for the servant knoweth not what his lord doeth: But I have called you friends; for all things that I have heard of my Father I have made known unto you."

John 15:15

"If it be possible, as much as lieth in you, live peaceably with all men."

Romans 12:18

"Salt is good: but if the salt have lost his saltness, wherewith will ye season it? Have salt in yourselves, and have peace one with another."

Mark 9:50

Dear God,

Give Pastor _____ the strength and wisdom to live peaceably with all men. Let your Holy Spirit be during every relationship Pastor _____ has. Allow Pastor _____ to maintain godly friendships. Open Pastor _____ eyes to see every relationship that is not of you and cancel it in Jesus' name. Thank you for Pastor _____. In Jesus name I pray, Amen.

Special Notes

"Pray Without Ceasing"
I Thessalonians 5:17

The Pastor's Leadership

The Pastor's Leadership

The pastor is called to lead the church in the path of God's plans. The pastor must understand that he will not be able to lead a congregation by himself, but needs support from people of many gifts and talents. The pastor's ability to delegate and identify the gifts of his congregation becomes crucial to the progress of any church.

Supporting Scriptures

"And Moses chose able men out of all Israel, and made them heads over the people, rulers of thousands, rulers of hundreds, rulers of fifties, and rulers of tens."

Exodus 18:25

"Take you wise men, and understanding, and known among your tribes and I will make them rulers over you."

Deuteronomy 1 :13

"For I have given you an example, that ye should do as I have done to you."

John 13 :15

Dear God,

Give wisdom and understanding to Pastor _____ to be able to lead our church towards your vision. Give Pastor _____ insight to identify the leaders and laypersons to fulfill your mission for our church. Always let Pastor _____ lead by example. Constantly open Pastor _____ eyes to see the task that should be released from him. Thank you for Pastor _____. In the name of Jesus, I pray, Amen.

Special Notes

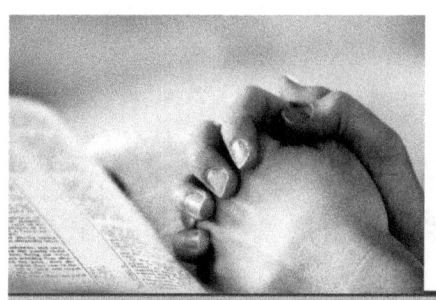

"Pray Without Ceasing"
I Thessalonians 5:17

The Pastor's Spiritual Guidance

The Pastor's Spiritual Guidance

The pastor will come in contact with a variety of issues and circumstances that face the congregants. The pastor must sit and listen to multiple problems on any given day. There are times when the pastor, perhaps, may not have experienced any of the issues that come through his door; but is able to provide his wisdom and compassion for any problem.

Supporting Scriptures

"He that answereth a matter before he heareth it, it is folly and shame unto him."

Proverbs 18:13

"Blessed be God, even the Father of our Lord Jesus Christ, the Father of mercies, and the God of all comfort. Who comforteth us in all our tribulation, that we may be able to comfort

them which are in any trouble, by the comfort wherewith we ourselves are comforted of God."
II Corinthians 1:3, 4

"And ye shall know the truth and the truth shall make you free."
John 8:32

Dear God,

Give Pastor _____ the wisdom to minister in any situation. Allow your compassion to always be present as Pastor _____ speaks life to hurting people. Give Pastor _____ a listening ear, even when he/she doesn't agree. Allow Pastor _____ to lead and guide according to your Word. Thank you for Pastor _____. In Jesus name I pray, Amen.

Special Notes

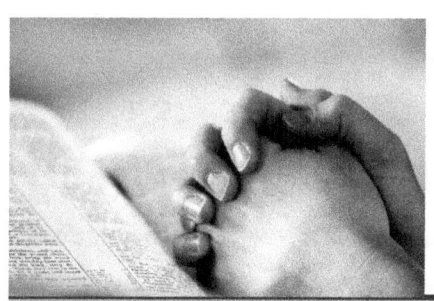

"Pray Without Ceasing"
I Thessalonians 5:17

The Pastor's Communication

The Pastor's Communication

The pastor must communicate to a variety of people daily (congregants, pastors, world leaders, state officials, banks, contractors, church leaders, organization leaders, family, friends, those in need, etc). The pastor not only must communicate effectively, but is always representing the Kingdom of God.

Supporting Scriptures

"Then the Lord put forth his hand, and touch my mouth. And the Lord said unto me, behold, I have put my words in thy mouth."

Jeremiah 1:9

"Let no corrupt communication proceed out of your mouth, but that which is good to the use of edifying, that it may minister grace unto the hearers."

Ephesians 4:29

"Let your speech be always with grace, seasoned with salt, that ye may know how ye ought to answer every man."

Colossians 4:6

Dear God,

I pray that Pastor _____ will allow you to place divine words in his/her mouth. I pray that his/her conversation be seasoned with grace. I pray that Pastor _____ communication is never corrupt, but ministers in grace always. Thank you for Pastor _____. In Jesus name I pray, Amen.

Special Notes

_____
_____
_____
_____
_____
_____
_____
_____
_____
_____
_____
_____
_____
_____
_____
_____
_____
_____
_____
_____
_____
_____
_____

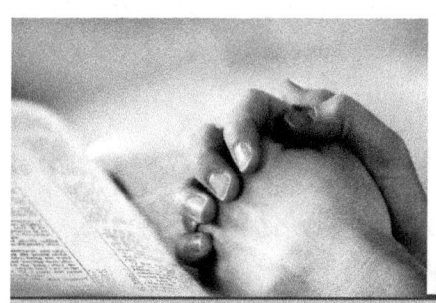

"Pray Without Ceasing"
I Thessalonians 5:17

The Pastor and God's Power

The Pastor and God's Power

Throughout Scripture, God has led men and women with His sovereignty. The pastor understands that there is no power above the almighty hand of God. The pastor must trust that God has complete control of all things.

Supporting Scriptures

"Ah Lord God! Behold, thou has made the heaven and the earth by thy great power and stretched out arm, and there is nothing too hard for thee."
Jeremiah 32:17

"For with God nothing shall be impossible."
Luke 1:37

"Is any thing too hard for the Lord? At the time appointed I will return unto thee, according to the time of life, and Sarah shall have a son."
Genesis 18:14

Dear God,

Manifest your power by the Holy Spirit through Pastor _____. Allow your signs and wonders to be displayed through Pastor _____. Allow Pastor _____ to never rely on his/her strength and power, but only on your power. Thank you for Pastor _____. In Jesus name I pray, Amen.

Special Notes

_____

_____

_____

_____

_____

_____

_____

_____

_____

_____

_____

_____

_____

_____

_____

_____

_____

_____

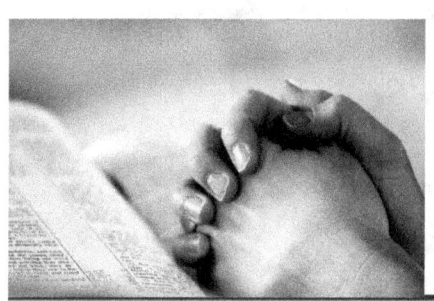

"Pray Without Ceasing"
I Thessalonians 5:17

The Pastor's Favor

The Pastor's Favor

The Bible is clear that favor can be found in God and man. God uses man to bless people. A pastor understands that his favor extends beyond the church walls.

Supporting Scriptures

"And Jesus increased in wisdom and stature, and in favour with God and man."

Luke 2:52

"And the child Samuel grew on, and was in favour both with the Lord, and also with men."

I Samuel 2:26

"When a man's ways please the Lord, he maketh even his enemies to be at peace with him."

Proverbs 16:7

Dear God

I pray your favor rests upon Pastor
_____ and his/her ministry all the
days of his/her life. Let Pastor _____
find favor in every encounter within and outside the
church. Let your favor be clear and unquestionable.
Thank you for Pastor _____. In Jesus
name I pray, Amen.

Special Notes

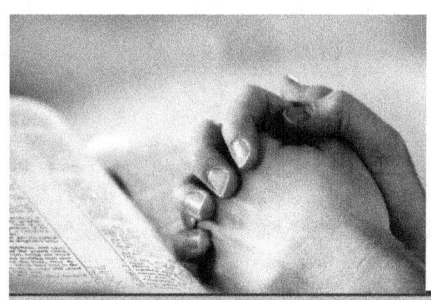

"Pray Without Ceasing"
I Thessalonians 5:17

The Pastor's Forgiveness

The Pastor's Forgiveness

Jesus died on the cross so that a world could have access to forgiveness. The pastor should approach forgiveness as Jesus did, and the example of forgiveness should be carried out in the church. Forgiveness becomes a door that releases the pastor from church hurt.

Supporting Scriptures

"Therefore if thou bring thy gift to the altar, and there rememberest that thy brother hath aught against thee. Leave there thy gift before the altar, and go thy way; first be reconciled to thy brother, and then come and offer thy gift."

Matthew 5:23, 24

"For if ye forgive men their trespasses, your heavenly Father will also forgive you."

Matthew 6:14

"So likewise shall my heavenly Father, do also unto you, if ye from your hearts forgive not everyone his brother their trespasses."
Matthew 18:35

Dear God,

Allow Pastor _____ to live a lifestyle of forgiveness. Let Pastor _____ be expedient in reconciliation when the need arises. Open Pastor _____ heart to forgive when he/she experiences the deepest of church hurt, whether it be from leaders, the community, or even the membership. Thank you for Pastor _____. In Jesus name I pray, Amen.

Special Notes

_____

_____

_____

_____

_____

_____

_____

_____

_____

_____

_____

_____

_____

_____

_____

_____

_____

_____

_____

"Pray Without Ceasing"
I Thessalonians 5:17

The Pastor and Covetousness

The Pastor and Covetousness

God has called each pastor to minister in certain vineyards for His glory and honor. God has entrusted to the pastor the parishioners under his care and to be faithful with the ministry God has ordained.

Supporting Scriptures

"And he said unto them, Take heed, and beware of covetousness: for a man's life consisteth not in the abundance of the things which he possesseth."
Luke 12:15

"Thou shalt not covet thy neighbor's house, thou shalt no covet thy neighbor's wife, nor his manservant, nor his ox, nor his ass, nor any thing that is thy neighbor's."
Exodus 20:17

"The prince that wanteth understanding is also a great oppressor; but he that hateth covetousness shall prolong his days."

Proverbs 28:16

Dear God,

I pray that Pastor _____ will be fulfilled in the ministry you have ordained for his/her life. Help Pastor _____ not to covet another pastor's ministry. Reaffirm Pastor _____ in this church. Close Pastor _____ ears to the voice of the enemy, that will take him/her out of your will. Thank you for Pastor _____. In Jesus name I pray, Amen.

Special Notes

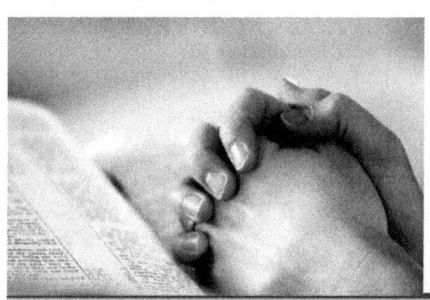

"Pray Without Ceasing"
I Thessalonians 5:17

The Pastor and God's Promises

The Pastor and God's Promises

The pastor must be fully persuaded that God will fulfill all His promises in his life and ministry. The pastor will stand on God's promises for his congregants.

Supporting Scriptures

"And being fully persuaded that, what he had promised, he was able also to perform."

Romans 4:21

"Being confident of this very thing that he which hath begun a good work in you will perform it until the day of Jesus Christ."

Philippians 1:6

"For all the promises of God in him are yea, and in him Amen, unto the glory of God by us."

II Corinthians 1:20

Dear God,

I pray that every word given to Pastor _____ will come to pass. God, you said that as the rain and dew fall to the ground and bud, so shall your Word come down. Continue to encourage Pastor _____ to trust in you and your Word. Thank you for Pastor _____. In Jesus name I pray, Amen.

Special Notes

"Pray Without Ceasing"
I Thessalonians 5:17

The Pastor's Calling

The Pastor's Calling

The call of a pastor is vital to the body of Christ and is crucial to kingdom building. The pastor must be sure of his calling, because he will be challenged.

Supporting Scriptures

"Therefore, the prisoner of the Lord, beseech you that ye walk worthy of the vocation wherewith ye are called."
Ephesians 4:1

"Wherefore the rather, brethren give diligence to make your calling and election sure: for if ye do these things, ye shall never fall."
II Peter 1:10

"Wherefore also we pray always for you, that our God would count you worthy of this calling, and fulfill all the good pleasure of his goodness, and the work of faith with power."
II Thessalonians 1:11

Dear God,

I pray that Pastor _____ will always walk worthy of the calling that you have placed on his/her life. Father God, in the name of Jesus, allow Pastor _____ to see the obstacles that may hinder his/her walk. Give Pastor _____ the wisdom necessary to avoid these obstacles. Let Pastor _____ always minister in the name of the Lord, his/her God. Thank you for Pastor _____. In Jesus name I pray, Amen.

Special Notes

"Pray Without Ceasing"
I Thessalonians 5:17

The Pastor's Joy

The Pastor's Joy

More than happiness, God wants the pastor
to experience His joy. The pastor understands
that joy will take him past the ups and downs
that happiness cannot bring.

Supporting Scriptures

*"Thou wilt show me the path of life: in thy
presence is fulness of joy..."*

Psalm 16:11

*"Then he said unto them, Go your way, eat the
fat, and drink the sweet, and send portions unto
them for whom nothing is prepared: for this day
is holy unto our Lord: neither be ye sorry; for the
joy of the Lord is your strength."*

Nehemiah 8:10

"These things have I spoken unto you, that my joy might remain in you, and that your joy might be full."

John 15:11

Dear God,

Fill Pastor _____ with your joy, and let your joy be his/ her very strength. Allow each day that Pastor _____ walks to be filled with your peace. Don't let the stress of ministry to take his/her joy, but let Pastor _____ remember that in You is all joy. Thank you for Pastor _____. In Jesus name I pray, Amen.

Special Notes

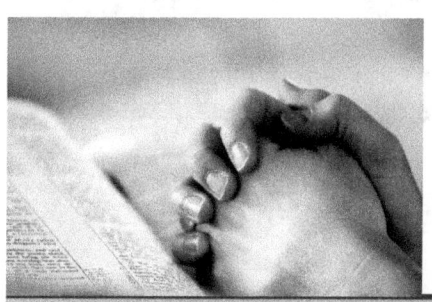

"Pray Without Ceasing"
I Thessalonians 5:17

The Pastor's Troubles

The Pastor's Troubles

The life of a pastor is filled with challenges as it pertains to the church, ministry, and family. The weight of the congregation can be very stressful. God wants the pastor to put all his troubles in His hand.

Supporting Scriptures

"Casting all your cares upon him; for he careth for you."

I Peter 5:7

"Cast thy burden upon the Lord, and he shall sustain thee: he shall never suffer the righteous to be moved."

Psalm 55:22

"Therefore I say unto you, take no thought for your life, what ye shall eat, or what ye shall drink; nor yet for your body, what ye shall put

on. Is not the life more than meat, and the body than raiment?"

Matthew 6:25

Dear God,

I pray that Pastor _____ will give you of all his/her troubles. Let not the weight of the church discourage Pastor _____. I pray that Pastor _____ will seek you first in all things when dealing with any trouble. Thank you for Pastor _____. In Jesus name I pray, Amen.

Special Notes

www.ingramcontent.com/pod-product-compliance
Lightning Source LLC
Chambersburg PA
CBHW071007120626
46546CB00003B/973